Love Your Kitten

GW00702900

Love Your Kitten

by Malcolm Welshman
B.V.Sc., M.R.C.V.S.

W. Foulsham & Co. Ltd.
London • New York • Toronto • Cape Town • Sydney

Page 2: A 6-month-old finds a comfortable bed

W. Foulsham & Company Limited
Yeovil Road, Slough, Berkshire, SL 1 4JH

ISBN 0–572–01368–X

Printed in Spain by Cayfosa. Barcelona
Dep. Leg. B-11515-1986

Contents

1 The Kitten as a Pet

You must first ask yourself why you want to own a kitten. That adorable bundle of fluff is quickly going to grow up. And cats live a long life. I know of several that are over 20 years old.

As the owner, you will be responsible for the kitten's feeding, grooming and health. This all costs money. Then what about your holidays? Arrangements will have to be made to have your cat boarded in a cattery or be looked after by friends.

And are there very small children in your home? This can create problems, as some youngsters may think of the kitten as just a toy to be pulled around by the tail. This can result in scratched faces and floods of tears. Kindness can be taught, but make sure you have the patience and the time. You will need to show your children how to lift and hold a kitten properly; and firmly discourage any ill treatment. That is quite a responsibility.

Then, there is the question of other pets in the house, especially dogs. Is the introduction of a kitten going to result in an all-out war? Hardly fair, if the opponent is a large, inquisitive Great Dane. In my experience, most dogs and cats eventually reach a truce. But in the

Kittens make great pets!

early stages, you will need to keep an eye open for likely skirmishes. If you do own a dog, it may be more sensible to choose an older cat instead.

But, providing you select the right cat – one that suits your needs and fits into your family environment – you will be rewarded with a clean, intelligent companion that will give you many hours of entertainment.

So do think carefully before you decide to have a kitten. Still keen? Then let us consider the best way to choose one.

Before we do that, a note for anyone who has received a kitten as a gift. This is not necessarily the best way to get a kitten, unless you have agreed on the gift beforehand and can be involved in the choice. But don't skip the next chapters. After all, you may find your cat is such a good companion that you will want another.

2 The Choice of Kitten

There really is no difference between a pedigree or an ordinary domestic cat. They both require the same amount of attention. You may think it more fun to own a pedigree cat from which you can breed or which you can take to shows. But, remember, such a cat is expensive to buy. Still, it could be worthwhile, since you will be getting the kitten from a reputable breeder who will have been careful to ensure the kitten's health and breeding records were of the highest standard. And you will know what your kitten will look like when it grows up. Unlike the ordinary household cat which might turn out quite different to what you expected.

Three main categories of pure-bred cats are recognised: long haired, British short haired and foreign short haired.

The long haired cats are often called Persians. They have long flowing coats and tails, rounded heads and short noses. Their eyes are very striking, being large and deep copper, orange or blue depending on coat colour.

The British short hairs have dense short coats. They are fairly compact animals with tails that are thick at the base and rounded at the tip. Their heads are rounded with small

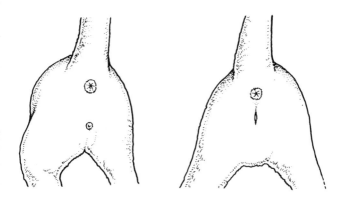

Sexing kittens: in the male, the urethral opening is like a small dot below the anus: in the female, the opening (vulva) is closer to the anus.

ears. They have short noses and large rounded eyes.

The foreign short hairs include some well-known breeds such as the Burmese and Siamese with their slanted eyes, and the Russian Blue and Abyssinian.

Once you have decided on the breed, you will need to consider the choice between a male or a female. The sex of your kitten should not be of prime importance since either one can be neutered. However, if you wish to keep your cat entire, there are certain problems of which you should be aware. These may influence your choice.

Females have regular heat periods or oestrous cycles. When in heat, they can be very vocal. This can annoy neighbours. And what happens to all the kittens produced? Thousands of unwanted youngsters are born every year. It is unresponsible pet ownership to allow a female cat to produce litter after litter.

Chinchilla kittens

Unneutered adult males are constantly on the roam for females in heat. They produce a strong smelling urine and are liable to spray their territory. This means your furniture and skirting boards. The resulting 'tom cat' atmosphere in your living room may be attractive to a female cat but will hardly endear you to your friends.

Remember, neutered cats still make friendly pets.

One last point. You may want to choose a long haired kitten in preference to a short haired variety. Fine. They often tend to be more docile. But, do bear in mind that the long haired cat requires frequent grooming. Without it, the coat gets tangled and the resultant knots can be impossible to remove. Then you will end up having to go to your vet to have the cat dematted under anaesthetic. Also, it is not such a good idea to have a long haired cat when there are small children around. The long hair seems to attract a constant stream of toffees, glue and sticky jam.

So, now you have made up your mind. You know the sort of kitten you would like. Let us consider the best place to buy one.

Silver Tabby (British)
Lilac Siamese and kittens

3 **Buying your Kitten**

If you have decided to buy a pure-bred kitten, try your local pet shops. These frequently sell pure-bred and ordinary domestic cats and they are usually less expensive than elsewhere. Or get in touch with a breeder through one of the cat organisations, or look through the advertisements in one of the cat magazines. There is a list of useful addresses in the back of the book. Failing that, contact your local veterinary surgeon. He may have several clients who breed cats. Another good idea is to visit one of the many cat shows held up and down the country. Here, you will find breeders exhibit their best kittens. Often they are for sale. If not, orders can be taken for later litters.

Do not forget another source of supply – the postcard in your newsagent's window. Many a sturdy British house cat has been found a good home in this way.

Finally, there are the rescue centres such as the RSPCA and the Cats' Protection League with kittens and adults crying out for adoption.

Abyssinian kittens
Russian Blue kittens

Now for some advice on the actual selection of your kitten. Take note of the pet shop or cattery's appearance. If it seems dirty and the cats' quarters are in poor condition and soiled, go elsewhere. Uncaring owners means uncared for cats. Never select an unhealthy kitten. You may feel sorry for it, but you are buying trouble. And do not be taken in by the cute little kitten. It is far more important to look for signs of good health.

Here is a check list to help you select the best kitten.

1. Look for the one that is alert, active and playful. The shy kitten often has a nervous disposition, making it unsuitable where there are small children in the family.

2. The kitten's eyes should be bright and clear with no soreness or discharge.

3. The nose should be clean though not necessarily cold.

4. There should be no brown, waxy material in the ears. This is often a sign of mites and the kitten will usually be shaking its head or scratching its ears.

5. Open the kitten's mouth. Teeth should be sharp and white, gums firm and pink. Look for any sores on the tongue.

6. Run your hands down the kitten's back to check that its body is well muscled with no lumps or bumps.

7. The coat should be free of mats and dandruff. Examine for fleas; a tell-tale sign is the presence of flea dirts – seen as black specks.

8. Lift the kitten's tail and look for pasting of the hair with faecal material – a sign of diarrhoea. Tiny white rice-like segments in this

Three-week old kittens

area indicates a tapeworm problem. Ask if the kitten has been wormed. Any faeces in the pen should be firm.

From this check list, does the kitten seem healthy? If so, it is yours for the asking. Now it is time to meet the family.

4 **Bringing the Kitten Home**

Before you bring your kitten home, you will need to plan ahead. First, consider the journey. Please do not try to cuddle the kitten on the back seat of the car. He may be frightened and leap off your lap. Worse still, he may be car sick. You need a suitable travelling basket or box and not a home-made one unless you are an expert handyman. There will be many occasions in the future when you will have to transport your cat. You will be surprised how clever cats can be at squeezing out of home-made carriers.

Cardboard containers such as those obtainable from welfare societies are adequate. They need air holes punched in the sides for ventilation. Do not be over enthusiastic in making these holes. Otherwise, with just a little frenzied gnawing and a helping paw, you will have a frightened cat tearing round the car.

Wicker baskets with a wire screen at the front are an improvement. But I prefer the plastic coated wire carriers. These are escape-proof and easily cleaned. Also the cat can see where he is going. A good pet shop or your veterinary surgeon should be able to provide you with such a basket.

When travelling, place the carrier on the

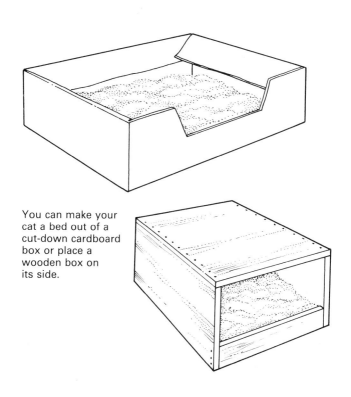

You can make your cat a bed out of a cut-down cardboard box or place a wooden box on its side.

floor of the car. This may help to prevent your kitten being sick. And talk to your new pet – lots of reassurance does help – but avoid the temptation to let the kitten out. That must wait until you are safely indoors.

You will need to provide sleeping quarters for your kitten. You could buy a commercial cat bed from your pet shop. A box or basket with a soft blanket is often a workable idea. Place this under the sideboard or in a corner. It should be somewhere your kitten can retreat to and feel protected.

For food and water, there are plenty of dishes from which to choose. It does not matter whether food dishes are plastic, or stainless steel providing they are unbreakable and easy to clean. Check on the design. A lightweight plastic saucer is unsuitable since it is easily overturned. Any dish should not be more than 5 cm (2 inches) high otherwise your kitten may be tempted to put his paws on the rim and tip his dinner over himself.

The best drinking bowls are earthenware. They are heavy and help to keep the water cool in hot weather.

Cats are clean animals and will not usually mess their beds or immediate surroundings. If they do start soiling the house it is more likely to be your fault for not having the necessary facilities. So make sure you provide a sanitary tray. This should be waterproof, preferably stainless steel or plastic and large enough for the cat to be able to turn round in it once he has grown up. Make sure the tray is at least 5 cm (2 inches) deep otherwise you will find litter being scratched onto the floor. Should you prefer to use disposable trays, treated cardboard varieties are available from pet shops.

Think carefully where you are going to put the tray. I suggest you place it near the kitten's bed. Then, when the kitten wakes up, he can use the tray straight away. It should not be moved from place to place. This will just confuse your kitten and he may stop using it. However, as your pet grows up, you may not want to have a sanitary tray in the house. Time, then, to move the tray gradually nearer to the back door until it is finally outside. But please make a tray available to start with.

Kittens need their own bed
Cat using tray

Litter trays should be waterproof, easy to clean and large enough to allow the cat to turn round. Some trays can be bought with a domed lid and a side entrance to give the cat privacy.

Otherwise, your kitten may use any odd corner of your house and become very unpopular.

You will need litter for the tray. This can be sand, peat moss, sawdust or commercial cat litter. The latter is better for long haired cats. If you bought your kitten from a breeder, ask what sort of litter was used. Provide the same and your kitten will soon realise what the tray is meant for. Supply sufficient litter to give a depth of 5 cm (2 inches) and keep the tray clean. Cats will not use a dirty sanitary tray and will go elsewhere. That means those odd corners of your house again.

All cats like playing with toys. Hard rubber balls, spools on a string and ping-pong balls will provide hours of entertainment for the kitten, and for you just watching his antics. But ensure the toys are safe and not likely to be chewed and swallowed.

As regards food, if the kitten is bought from a breeder, get a diet sheet in advance. This will show the kinds of food the kitten is used to. Then food for the first few days can be bought before the kitten arrives.

The kitten's first day in your home is extremely important. He has to adapt to lots of new smells, sounds and people, so treat your kitten with care. Let him have a sniff round. But make sure there are no escape routes such as open windows. And do not forget the fire-

To hold a kitten correctly, place one hand under his chest with his front legs between your fingers. Support the hindquarters with the other hand.

place. The last thing you need is the fire brigade rescuing your kitten from half way up the chimney.

Everyone will want to handle the kitten, but be patient and wait until the kitten has settled in. Then be sure to handle him correctly. Place one hand under the kitten's chest, holding the front legs between your fingers and support the hindquarters with the other hand. If not held correctly the kitten may become frightened, wriggle and scratch. The result? One dropped kitten with a possible broken leg.

Watch out for your other pets. They will be extremely interested in the new arrival. But let the introductions wait until your kitten has adjusted to his new environment.

Once the kitten has had a good look round, leave him in the room where you have put his bed, tray and toys. There may be a few plaintive meows but the sight of a bowl of warm milk should put a stop to that. And soon your kitten will be lapping up his life as a member of your family.

5 **Feeding**

Correct feeding means a healthy cat. Your kitten will depend on you to provide the right sort of food. This diet must contain the correct proportions of protein, fat, carbohydrates, vitamins and minerals.

Protein found in meat and fish is essential for growth and repair. It is important to realise that cats require much more protein than dogs. Fat is a source of energy and helps to keep the cat's skin and hair in good condition. The fatty acids found in vegetable oils are especially important in ensuring a sleek, glossy coat. Carbohydrates found in vegetables and cereals also provide energy. But cats do not find it easy to digest raw carbohydrates and so if vegetables or cereals are offered they should be cooked. Tiny amounts of minerals are required in the diet. Of special importance are calcium and phosphorus to ensure healthy teeth and sound bones. Vitamins are also essential to ensure your kitten remains healthy, but, again, they are only required in very small amounts. Your kitten will need vitamin A, high quantities of which are found in liver, vitamin D found in cod liver oil, and the B vitamins, a rich source of which is yeast. If you feed your kitten a well balanced diet, this will contain everything to keep him healthy.

Fresh Foods

The cat, being a carnivorous animal, requires meat, but this should only form part of the daily food intake. Suitable meats which can be given raw are muscle meat (beef, lamb, chicken, rabbit), liver (beef, lamb, chicken), hearts, kidneys (beef, lamb). Pork should only be given if cooked. Fish must be cooked and the bones removed or the fish minced.

You can cook the meat if you wish. It will be less likely to cause digestive upsets. If you do feed raw meat, cats like to eat it at room temperature, so take it out of the refrigerator in good time.

Do not feed an exclusive diet of lean meat such as minced beef or heart, since these foods contain insufficient calcium for your cat's needs. Likewise, too much fish can result in a deficiency of thiamin (one of the B vitamins) and vitamin E and cause ill health.

But what if your cat is a fussy eater, preferring to eat tasty things like liver and kidneys? You must discourage this as it is an unbalanced diet. Liver and kidneys are nutritious but must be fed in combination with other foods.

You may find your cat likes vegetables. Cooked spinach, runner beans, carrots, rice and tomatoes are fine. Go easy on cooked potatoes as your cat may put on too much weight.

Cheese and the occasional egg can be given to vary the diet but they are not essential. Some cats cannot tolerate egg white so just feed the yoke or hard-boil the egg for easier digestion.

Feeding time — Red, Tortoiseshell, Red, Blue

Milk

Do not assume your kitten must have milk. Some cats do not like it. Occasionally it can cause diarrhoea. If this happens, try diluting the milk with water or substitute skimmed or powdered milk.

Canned Foods

There are many canned foods on the market and besides being convenient to give are both palatable and nutritious. The manufacturers have ensured that a balanced meal is provided. There is a wide choice of flavours, some combined with cereals, others just plain meat or fish. So alternate one variety with another to avoid monotony of diet.

Dry Foods

There are a number of dry cat foods available similar in consistency to dog biscuits. They contain cereals, vitamins and minerals flavoured with beef, chicken, lamb or fish.

Not all cats like them. But most enjoy something to crunch on, and it is good for their teeth. Some cats become addicted to them, refusing to eat other foods. This could be harmful. So only feed as part of a balanced diet and make sure plenty of water is available when you give the food.

Bones

It is not a good idea to allow your cat to have bones. There is always a danger that a piece could become wedged in the mouth or lodged in the intestines. So cut the meat from chop bones and make sure all fish bones are removed. This also applies to chicken bones which, if eaten, can splinter and the sharp edges perforate the intestines.

Yes, I know cats eat birds, bones and all. But it is the cooking of bones which makes them brittle and liable to splinter. So throw all bones in the dustbin. But make sure the lid is on tight!

Vitamin and Mineral Supplements

These are only necessary in special circumstances. It is easy to do harm by over zealous supplementation.

Kittens and growing cats should receive additional vitamins and minerals in tablet or powder form, fed according to the manufacturer's instructions. This will ensure adequate intake of vitamins especially A and D and provide the correct ratio of calcium and phosphorus for sound growth of the kitten's bones.

Pregnant and nursing animals will also require supplementation of their diet. Otherwise, if your cat is on a well balanced, mixed diet there is no need to worry about extra vitamins and minerals.

Water

Ensure that fresh drinking water is always available. Your cat may only take the occasional lap, obtaining most of his water requirements from the food. But at least the water should be there if required.

Grass

All cats like to eat grass at some time or other, so provide them with access to it. If you have no garden, then grow some in a pot or window box. Long haired cats especially benefit from eating grass since it helps them to bring up any fur they may have swallowed while grooming themselves.

Avoid obtaining grass from parks or gardens which may have been sprayed with poisonous chemicals.

Feeding Programme

Cats are creatures of habit so it is best to feed them at the same time and in the same place each day. Then you will probably find your cat will queue up for his meal and be less likely to pester you at other times of the day. Put the food down for 20 minutes – long enough for him to eat it. If he leaves it, take it away and do not offer any more until the next regular meal time. If it is still refused, repeat the procedure. Your cat will soon learn.

A kitten has a tiny stomach and so can only eat small quantities of food. When you first bring him home, your kitten will probably be between eight and twelve weeks old. He should be on four meals a day. Take note of the breeder's diet, if one has been provided, and follow this to begin with.

In general, the following feeding regime should be satisfactory. For breakfast, give a heaped tablespoonful of meat varying it between tinned kitten food and minced beef, fish, chicken or rabbit. At lunchtime, provide the kitten with as much milk and cereal as he wants. At teatime, repeat the meat meal but add a pinch of vitamin and mineral supplement. Then round off the evening with another milky meal. Gradually increase the amount of food and supplement according to what the kitten will eat at any one time. There are no exact amounts. You will have to be the judge of that. When the kitten reaches four months of age, you can reduce the feeds to three a day, leaving out the evening milky meal. Throughout this period avoid any sudden changes in diet. This is especially important with young kittens. Introduce new foods gradually to prevent digestive upsets.

By eight months of age, your cat will only need to have two good quality meals a day. Some animals only eat once a day. Find out what your cat prefers and feed accordingly. If your cat starts to put on weight, cut down on

Blue long-haired
Short haired silver tabby
Blue long hair with Birman

the amount of food with no titbits between meals. An obese cat is not a healthy cat, so keep your pet slim and sleek.

And do not forget to provide a variety of foods. Cats soon get used to one type of food and then resent change. But persevere. Your cat may not eat for a couple of days but eventually will give in. It is important to have several foods that you know your cat will eat. Then, if ever he becomes ill, you will have several different diets with which to tempt him.

You will know if you are feeding your cat correctly by his appearance. He will be sleek with a glossy coat and supple skin. Whenever you catch his eye, you will see that dreamy, contented look that comes from a cat well fed.

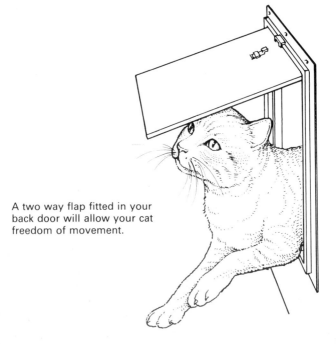

A two way flap fitted in your back door will allow your cat freedom of movement.

6 **General Care**

Grooming

All cats need grooming. Your kitten will be no exception. Every breed sheds hair, especially in the autumn and spring. But as many cats now spend most of their time indoors under artificial light, hair will be shed constantly, so there is always a need for grooming.

Start as soon as you get your kitten. This will ensure that he becomes used to being handled. Also, at this age, you will have better control of him. Any attempt to play, claw, bite or dash off should be stopped at once. Be firm and do not give in. Place the kitten back where you were grooming him and start again.

You will need a metal comb with teeth wide set at one end, close set at the other, a stiff brush, a pair of blunt ended scissors and a soft cloth or smoothing glove.

Put your kitten on a table. Run the comb through the hair against the lie of the coat. Then reverse the procedure, and comb with the lie of the coat. If there are mats, tease these out using the wide-toothed end of the comb. You may be able to tease out the tangles with your fingers. If this fails, pull the mats away from the kitten's skin and snip the tangles off with the scissors. Do not forget to groom your cat all over. This will include the stomach area,

Kittens should be groomed regularly

under the legs and between the toes and pads. Use the fine teeth on the comb for the shorter hair on the head.

Once the hair has been combed out, brush with a good stiff brush. With long haired cats, brushing the hair against the way it grows will make it fluffy. With short haired cats, always work the coat in the direction in which it grows.

Finally, use a soft cloth in the same direction. Now your cat's coat will gleam. And remember, regular grooming will help to stop hair being shed all over your furniture and clothes.

Claws

You will need to check your cat's claws regularly. These will be needle sharp in a kitten and he may get caught up in the carpet, damaging his leg in the struggle to get free. You can clip your kitten's nails with special clippers bought from the pet shop. First press above and below

Clipping a kitten's nails

each toe with your finger and thumb. This will unsheath the claw. You will then be able to see a pink blood vessel, the quick, running down the centre of the claw. Snip carefully below the quick to avoid bleeding. If the claw does bleed, use a styptic pencil to stop the flow of blood. If a ragged edge is left, smooth off with sandpaper. Only the front claws need be trimmed.

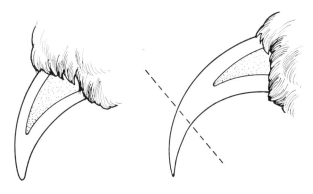

Claws should be cut below the quick to prevent bleeding.

You could provide your cat with a scratching post. Nail a log to a heavy wooden base or cover a post in carpet. You may still find your cat likes scratching the furniture, however, so keep an eye on those claws.

Eyes and Ears

Your cat's eyes and ears should be examined at each grooming session. A slight discharge in the inner corner of the eye is common in long haired cats. Wipe it away with damp cotton wool. Occasionally hair near the eyes curls in and can be a source of irritation. Carefully clip the hair away with blunt-ended scissors.

Now have a look inside your cat's ears. If they are clean, resist the temptation to poke around. The lining of the ear is very sensitive and you could cause a lot of pain. You may

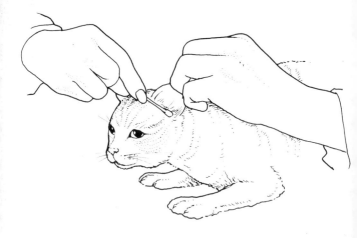

Excess wax can be cleared out of your cat's ears using a cotton bud dipped in mineral oil.

Tortoiseshell and white
A one-year-old investigating a flower pot

notice some reddish brown material. This is an accumulation of wax. It may be due to ear mites, in which case veterinary treatment is required. You can clean out small traces of wax on the inner surfaces of the ear flap and at the top of the ear canal. Use a cotton bud dipped in mineral oil or glycerine. Gently wipe the affected areas but do not probe down the ear.

Teeth

Once a week, check your cat's mouth and teeth. In seven to nine month old kittens the baby, or milk teeth may not be shed and so cause the permanent teeth to erupt out of position. This requires veterinary attention. Keep a look out for any inflammation of the gums and ulceration of the tongue. In older cats, there is a problem with food collecting between the teeth. This leads to the formation of tartar along the gum margins. Any build-up should be removed by your veterinary surgeon otherwise it can lead to dental disease and loss of teeth.

Bathing

Once in a while your cat may get really dirty. He may crawl under the car and get oil and grease on his coat. Then a bath will be necessary. Unfortunately, most cats hate being bathed so, in order to avoid having a fight on your hands, you should make all preparations in advance. The best place for bathing is in the kitchen sink with a draining board. Have ready a plastic cup for pouring water over your cat,

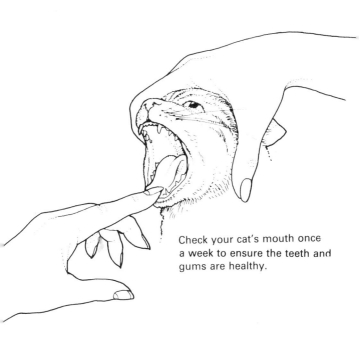

Check your cat's mouth once a week to ensure the teeth and gums are healthy.

mild baby shampoo, warm, dry towels and a basket to put the cat in to ensure he does not escape wet and bedraggled. Some cats tolerate a hair drier, so have one ready just in case.

Place a rubber mat or towel in the sink and similar on the draining board. Cats hate to feel their feet slipping. Fill the sink with 7–10 cm (3 to 4 inches) of lukewarm water. Plug the cat's ears with cotton wool to prevent water getting in. Hold the cat on the draining board and gently pour water over him using the plastic cup. Continue doing this until the hair is wet. Work in the shampoo and talk reassuringly. You may now be able to put the cat into the sink to rinse him. To do this, grasp him by the nape of the neck with one hand and, supporting the hindquarters with the other hand, lift the cat into the sink. Make sure you remove all traces of shampoo.

Your cat should be dried as much as possible with warm towels. Rub vigorously, making sure the hair next to the skin is thoroughly dried. If you have someone to help you, let them hold the cat while you try using a hair drier. If your cat dislikes this, keep him shut in a warm room until completely dry. It may be best to bath the cat in the evening and keep him indoors overnight. Once dry, give him a good comb since there will be a lot of loose hair. Comb or snip out any tangles.

What should you do if your cat gets paint on himself? If the paint is still wet, try removing with a cloth soaked in turpentine. But avoid contact with the cat's skin. If the paint has dried, clip out the affected area. You could try a little linseed oil to soften the paint which, once loosened, could be combed out.

Occasionally, cats get tar on their paws. This can be removed with paraffin but, as it irritates the skin, shampoo the paws immediately afterwards.

7 Your Kitten's Health

When you bought your kitten, he should have been bright eyed, active and healthy. However, he may not always remain that way. One day, he might get injured or feel off colour. He cannot tell you when he is ill. It is your responsibility to be observant. Here is a list to help you know when your cat is not feeling very well.

1. Not wanting to eat or only finishing half of his food.

A sick cat has a poor appetite or none at all. Refusal to eat does not always mean the cat is ill. He may have been successful at catching mice or a friendly neighbour may have given him a saucerful of cream. Still, if your cat is off his food for more than two days, take that as a sign of something wrong.

2. Lying around, listless.

A cat in good health is alert, active and playful. A sick cat is very different. He will be reluctant to move around, perhaps just sitting in a hunched position with his eyes closed.

3. Dull, dry coat.

When a cat is ill, it oftens affects his skin and coat, turning glossy, sleek fur into dull hair which is shed all over the place.

4. Diarrhoea, constipation.

A healthy cat's bowel movements are regular and formed. Any change is indicative of a problem.

5. Frequent urination, straining, inability to urinate.

6. Bad breath

Normally, your cat's breath will have no odour. But remember, a fishy meal will change all that for a day.

7. Chronic coughing and sneezing.

Your cat may occasionally cough or sneeze when he gets a bit of hair or fluff up his nose. But watch out for continuous sneezing especially if accompanied by a discharge from the eyes and nose.

8. Constant scratching at head and ears.

This may be a sign of mites causing irritation within the ears.

9. Wounds.

Although cats are very agile, it is surprising how often they can have an accident on a sharp object such as a jagged piece of glass from a broken greenhouse or come to blows with the local tom cat. The resulting gash or bite may go unnoticed until the cat become lame or a swelling develops.

10. Vomiting.

The occasional bit of hair or froth brought up is no cause for alarm, but persistant vomiting is serious.

11. Excessive thirst.

Any of these alterations in your cat's health should be taken seriously. If in the slightest doubt you should contact your veterinary surgeon for advice and treatment.

Two-week old kittens
Cream long haired kittens

Safeguarding your Kitten's Health

Vaccination

There are two conditions caused by viruses which can make your kitten extremely ill and can often prove fatal. These are feline infectious enteritis and cat flu.

In feline infectious enteritis, the onset is often sudden with a great deal of vomiting. The cat is very depressed and may cry out with pain. There may be diarrhoea. In the latter stages of the disease, the cat becomes depressed. He can die within a few days of onset of symptoms despite every effort to save his life.

Cat flu or feline influenza is caused by two viruses. Symptoms are loss of appetite, depression, sneezing, discharge from the eyes and nose and coughing. Ulcers on the tongue often make the cat salivate. Though adult cats can recover from flu, kittens may go down with pneumonia. This can prove fatal.

Fortunately, you can have your kitten vaccinated against these conditions. Initially, your kitten will have some immunity from his mother providing she has been vaccinated. But this immunity gradually decreases leaving your kitten exposed to infection. So have your kitten vaccinated between eight and twelve weeks of age. There will be a follow-up injection about three weeks later. Your veterinary surgeon will advise you about this. He will also tell you about the booster injections required each year and will provide you with a vaccination certificate.

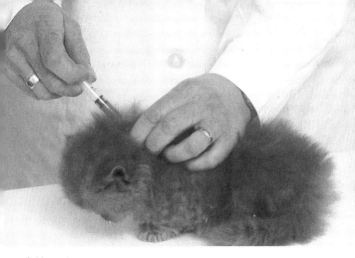

A kitten being vaccinated

Worming

There are two groups of worm seen in the cat: tapeworms and roundworms.

Infection with roundworms can be dangerous to young kittens. Worm eggs are picked up by contact with infected faeces though kittens can be born already infected from their mother. The larvae which hatch out are carried to the lungs. From here they eventually find their way back into the intestines where they mature into the adult worms. An infected kitten will be slow growing with a distended abdomen, poor coat and possibly diarrhoea. He will be thin despite a ravenous appetite. Occasionally, adult worms, brown-cream coloured and 7 to 10 cm (3 to 4 inches) long will be vomited. Pneumonia may result from the passage of larvae through the lungs. Large numbers of worms can cause blockage of the intestinal tract.

There is a slight risk to humans. A child, when playing with a kitten, may get worm eggs on his hands. These eggs could be swallowed and the larvae hatch out to wander round the child's body, eventually to lodge somewhere like the back of the eye where damage could be done.

So it is important to worm your kitten. If bought from a breeder he will have been wormed at four weeks of age. Ensure this is repeated at eight, twelve and sixteen weeks of age. Continue monthly until your kitten is six months old and then dose him every three months. Your veterinary surgeon will advise you on the best preparation to use.

The tapeworm does not cause so many problems. In the adult cat, you may not see any obvious symptoms but sometimes the worm causes digestive upsets, anaemia and nervous signs. Worm segments containing eggs are passed out with the cat's faeces. The segments may be seen as tiny rice-like grains round the fur under the tail or on the cat's bedding. Effective drugs to deal with these can be obtained from your veterinary surgeon.

Flea Control

Fleas are carriers of tapeworm larvae. Your cat could re-infect himself by swallowing such a flea. So flea control measures are necessary as part of the treatment for tapeworms. Fleas themselves can be a nuisance to your cat and may even be a nuisance to you since they will give you the occasional bite. And if you are allergic to flea bites you can become very itchy and sore. So can your cat. One bite may cause a massive skin reaction.

Fleas do not actually breed on the cat so you may not find any on your pet. But you should spot the flea dirts. These are tiny black specks found at the base of the hairs. Moisten one of these specks with water and a reddish stain will develop due to the digested blood they contain.

Treatment involves killing any fleas on the body using an insecticidal powder, spray or flea collar. These can be purchased from a good pet shop. But make sure the one you buy is suitable for use on cats. Apply a little spray or powder to the root of the tail and then to the back of the head and neck. Take care to avoid the face. Rub the powder gently into the fur. Now treat along the back and flanks. Stop the cat from licking himself for as long as possible. Then comb out any powder and, hopefully, dead fleas as well.

Flea collars can be effective, lasting for about three months at a time. But watch out for any inflammation to the skin around the collar since some cats can be allergic to the insecticide.

Besides treating your cat, you will need to treat places where the flea eggs may hatch. This means carpets, skirting boards and favourite places where your cat likes to sit. If you fail to do this, your cat will become reinfected. And make sure all susceptible pets in the household are treated.

Home Nursing

Nursing often has to be undertaken at home especially if the cat has an infectious disease liable to spread to other animals if he is kept in a veterinary hospital. Giving the right kind of care can often make all the difference to the outcome of an illness. You can help to boost the cat's morale, make him feel better and give him a will to live. However, continual fussing is to be avoided since an ill animal seeks solitude and peace. So do not overdo the nursing care!

The room where you keep him should be warm with adequate ventilation but free of draughts. It should be dry, with an absence of bright lights and noise, so not in the living room next to the TV, please. The cat's bed should be comfortable. A cardboard box with a soft blanket in it would be ideal and perhaps include a well wrapped up hot water bottle.

The sanitary tray should be within easy reach. Have two so that they can be changed over frequently. Most cats will adapt to using a tray even if they usually go outside.

Drinking water should always be available. If vomiting is a problem, glucose or barley water can be tried.

When a cat has been ill and off his food, you may find it difficult to start him eating again even though he may be feeling better. Cats have a well developed sense of smell so try tempting him with strongly smelling titbits such as sardines or liver sausage. You could try placing a morsel of his favourite food in his mouth or smearing some on his nose. He may lick it off and then start eating. Leave his food near him overnight. Some cats prefer eating in the dark when no-one is around. Never attempt to force feed your cat as this will exhaust and distress him.

Keep your cat clean. He may be too ill to do it himself. This is especially important with long haired cats. Cut away any matted or soiled hair. Keep grooming to a minimum, bearing in mind the cat is feeling ill. Wipe away any discharges with diluted, warm antiseptic such as TCP or use a warm salt solution. Wash soiled hair under the tail. Dry with soft towelling and apply talcum powder. Do all this very gently but quickly so that it does not upset your cat too much.

Your veterinary surgeon may have prescribed medication. This can be in liquid or tablet form. If there is a prolonged struggle in administration then it is better to take your cat to the surgery for injections. Before attempting to medicate, you will need to know how to hold your cat correctly. Sit him on a table and get someone to hold the cat's body between the forearms. Get the cat's hindquarters wedged against the helper and have one front leg of the cat held in each hand. The helper needs to maintain a firm grip because, if the cat feels himself being controlled, he is less likely to wriggle. If this method fails, sit the cat on a large towel or blanket, bring the long edge up under the cat's chin, holding onto the scruff and wrap the blanket tightly round the animal, tucking in any loose ends. The bundled up cat can be held in the helper's forearms, keeping a firm grip on the towel round the neck.

Liquid medicines, unless palatable, will just

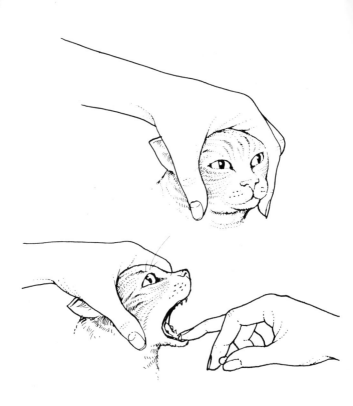

To give your cat a pill, hold his head firmly with your left hand, thumb and forefinger under the cheek bones. With the tablet between your right forefinger and thumb, use your middle finger to press down his lower jaw.

make your cat salivate. Pills are easier to give. With the cat firmly controlled, hold his head in your left hand, thumb and first finger under the cheek bones. Tilt the head back, stretching the neck a little. Liquid medicines can be poured from a dropper into the side of the mouth through the teeth. Give a little at a time and allow the cat to swallow. If a tablet is being given, hold it between right forefinger and thumb and use your middle finger to press down the lower jaw between the teeth. Then, with the head still tilted back, pop the tablet down the throat as far as you can. Hold the mouth firmly closed until the cat swallows. If the pill is spat out, try again. If you have no success, try crushing the tablet in some butter and smearing it on the teeth. This will not work with a pill tasting bitter since this makes the cat salivate.

First Aid

There may be occasions when prompt action by yourself will help to save your cat's life.

The animal involved in a road accident will be in a state of shock and probably injured. Take care in approaching him as he is liable to lash out if in pain. Cover with a thick blanket, roll up gently and pop in a travelling basket or other suitable container. Seek immediate veterinary treatment. Do not attempt anything yourself unless there is severe haemorrhage and an obvious bleeding point, in which case, apply pressure with a wad of cotton wool and bandage tightly.

Cats can be poisoned by eating a poisoned rat or mouse or chewing grass sprayed with chemicals. If you suspect your cat has just eaten something poisonous then make him sick by pushing a small lump of washing soda down his throat or giving strong salt solution. Seek immediate veterinary treatment.

Injuries inflicted by fighting with other cats can often lead to abscesses. If you have seen or heard your cat being involved in a quarrel, examine him carefully afterwards. Puncture

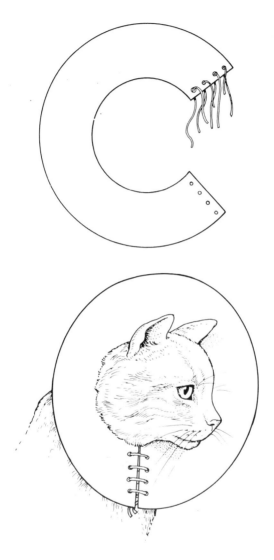

An Elizabethan collar will prevent a cat from biting at his stitches or licking at sore areas.

wounds from teeth or claws are often difficult to locate especially in long haired cats. But a tell-tale sign is often a tuft of damp hair where a spot of blood or serum has oozed out. Clip the hair round the area, bath with warm, diluted disinfectant and apply antibiotic ointment. Keep a careful eye on the wound and if any swelling and soreness develops then veterinary attention will be required.

Bones can occasionally become lodged in your cat's mouth. Make sure cooked fish, rabbit and chicken have the bones removed before feeding. A bone jammed across the back teeth will cause the cat to claw at his mouth and salivate. Restrain as for pill administration and look in his mouth. You may be able to pull the bone out with tweezers. A bone stuck down the throat will cause the cat to gag. There will be strings of saliva hanging from his mouth and he will refuse all food. This requires veterinary intervention.

Your cat may cut himself. Small cuts will heal without stitching. But some cats continually lick their wounds. If this happens your cat will need an Elizabethan collar. This can be made out of pliable cardboard with holes through which you lace some string. The collar is then tied round your cat's neck. But be warned, some cats go mad in their efforts to remove such collars. If this happens, you may have to try bandaging the affected area.

Whatever happens, your veterinary surgeon is always at hand. So if in doubt, seek professional advice. It may save your cat's life.

8 **Breeding**

Many owners like the idea of their cat having kittens, but think carefully first. You will need plenty of time to cope with the kittening and weaning. Suitable accommodation is required, well ventilated with plenty of warmth. And will you be able to find a home for all those kittens? If your pet is pure-bred, that may be quite easy. But it can be a worry finding good homes for ordinary moggies no matter how adorable those bundles of fur seem to be. If you are uncertain, have your cat speyed. But if you have decided that you are able and willing to look after a breeding female, read on.

Females have their first heat or oestrous cycle at about eight months of age. They will have several oestrous cycles in succession. If they are mated and become pregnant, these cycles stop. Each heat period lasts three to four days when the male is about, ten days or so if if he is not. There is a two to three week period of calm between heats. Climate has a bearing on when the heats occur. They are most common during summer and autumn, though cats living permanently indoors will cycle throughout the year.

You will soon know when your cat is in heat. She will become far more affectionate, rubbing herself incessantly against your legs. Stroke her and she will crouch and raise her tail. She will yowl and may even roll over and quiver. In fact, you may think she going to have a fit. Mind you, some individuals play shy, reserving their attentions for the one that matters – the roaming tom cat. There, the courtship will take place out-of-doors. But if you have a pedigree cat, make sure her attentions are directed to a proper stud. At least, then, you will know what sort of kittens to expect. All this must be organised in advance.

Long before your breeding female or queen is likely to call, you must decide which stud cat you wish to mate her to. Arrangements must be made with the owner since your cat will have to stay for a few days. This will allow her to settle down before being mated. Even then, your queen may not conceive. When she comes home, confine her indoors for a couple of days until you are certain she has stopped calling.

The Pregnant Cat

Good care during pregnancy will contribute to a healthy litter of kittens. Early on, begin feeding a nourishing diet, clear any skin problems, eliminate fleas and worms.

The average pregnancy lasts 61 to 63 days. If you know the day of mating and your cat is four days overdue, it is time to consult your veterinary surgeon.

After the first month of pregnancy, give your cat three meals a day, plus milk and a vitamin-mineral supplement containing plenty of calcium. Not until the fifth week of pregnancy will your cat start to become visibly swollen. By eight weeks, milk usually begins to appear in the mammary glands. They swell and the teats become encrusted with droplets of milk. This development becomes very pronounced during the last few days. Your cat will groom herself constantly, busily smoothing the hair away from the teats.

You should decide well in advance of the kittening which room is going to be the cat nursery. Box off a corner or clear out a cupboard. Better still provide a kittening box, 0.6 metres (2 feet) square and 0.6 metres (2 feet) on three sides. Make the fourth side only 15 cm (about 6 inches) high to enable the mother to get in and out while keeping the kittens in the nest. Your cat will probably make her nest many times over. Provide newspaper for her to tear up and make sure a sanitary tray is situated near at hand.

Near the time of delivery, she will become very restless, wandering about and scratching at her bed. She may even decide to have her kittens in some awkward place like a drawer or out in the garage, so keep an eye on her. In the last 12 hours before the kittens are due, she may lose her appetite.

When your cat goes into labour, leave her alone. Most kittens are born without assistance. However, a cat experiencing her first labour pains may be alarmed and leap out of the nesting box and dash round the room. If this happens, put her back in the box and stroke her to calm her down. Then just watch from a distance. The contractions will speed up, becoming more regular. Within two hours a kitten should be born. You will first see a little bloodstained fluid, followed by a greenish brown bubble and then the kitten's head. If the hindlegs appear first, this could cause prob-

Mother with 3-week-old kittens
A cream long haired cat with 2-week-old kittens

lems. Here you can help by grasping the legs with a towel and gently pulling as the cat contracts.

The kitten may still be enclosed in a transparent sac — the foetal membranes. The mother will free the kitten from these membranes and chew through the cord connecting the kitten to them. She will usually eat the afterbirth. If not, remove and dispose of it.

Sometimes, the mother does not break the membranes. In such a case, pick the kitten up and break the membranes away from the head. The kitten should then gasp for air. Wipe away any mucus around the nose and let the mother lick the kitten clean.

Even after the first kitten has been born, there is no guarantee that the others will follow quickly. Usually, though, they arrive within 10 to 15 minutes of each other and, if all is well, the mother will be nursing from three to five kittens within two hours.

She may be so absorbed with her new family that she refuses to eat for up to 24 hours. To encourage her, put a saucer of warm milk near her. Once she does start to eat then her normal food supplemented with vitamins and minerals will be sufficient. However, extra milk should always be provided.

Care of the Kittens

Leave the new family alone for two to three days and avoid unnecessary handling. Those kittens cannot see or hear for the first ten days and they find difficulty in crawling about. If they stray too far from mum, they will soon kick up a fuss, demanding warmth and food.

Check that they do not wander too far and make sure each kitten is getting enough milk. The more robust kittens will keep suckling the rear teats where the most milk is to be found. Ensure all the kittens get their fair share by rotating them on these rear teats. At the beginning there is a lot of fumbling and weaving about before a kitten manages to grasp a teat. But within 12 hours he will have learnt how to hang on and get himself a good feed. Mother will help with plenty of licking and nuzzling.

Kittens not getting enough to eat become thin, weak and will constantly cry. Such a kitten needs bottle feeding. This is easy to do as kittens have a natural urge to suck. You can buy cat fostering kits or use a baby doll's bottle. Newborn kittens need feeding every two hours for a couple of days, reducing this to every three to four hours. They will take up to 25 drops at a time. A proprietary brand of cat fostering milk can be used. Failing that, unsweetened evaporated milk or babies' powdered milk mixed up at double strength are adequate substitutes.

At about two to three weeks of age, the kittens will take their first tottering steps. Within days they will be tumbling about and playing. By four weeks they will have learnt to lap. By five weeks, the mother will start to wean her kittens off. She will reduce the number of feeds allowed, spend more time away from the kittens and introduce them to solid foods. You can help by providing raw minced beef, baby cereals and vegetables or use a proprietary tinned kitten food.

By the time they are six weeks of age, the kittens can be safely weaned from their mother and put on the feeding regime outlined in Chapter 5. Once the kittens are weaned, do not allow them to suckle the mother. Help her own milk to dry up by cutting down on the number of her meals and stop giving her milk to drink.

Weaned kittens will soon learn to use a sanitary tray if you place it near their sleeping quarters, gradually moving the tray away a short distance at a time. Handle the kittens as much as possible and get them used to being groomed. Once weaned, you will need to find the kittens good homes as soon as possible. Otherwise you may get too fond of them and want to keep them all.

9 **Showing**

If you are proud of your cat then why not show him off to other people? You will find it great fun. The local church fête may be a good starting point. But if you are more serious and have a pedigree animal, then you should consider one of the 50 or more cat shows held annually in Britain. Who knows, you may end up winning a prize.

First, you will need to know what shows are available to enter. Your kitten's breeder may be able to help. If you have joined a breed club, then the secretary will provide the necessary information. Failing that, a list of shows are published in the various cat magazines, the addresses of which can be found on page 64.

Choose your show carefully. To begin with, it is probably better to exhibit at a small, local exemption show. Check the date. A cat may not be shown twice in 14 days. This means you cannot show your cat two weeks running.

Study the rules carefully before filling in the entry form. You will need to give your cat's name, parentage, date of birth, registration number, breeder's name, the classes you have chosen to enter and your membership of any cat club. Send the form off with the entry forms well in advance of the closing date, otherwise you may find all the places have been taken.

Do not be put off by the large number of classes. Your cat can enter 12. I would advise you to enter only three or four to start with just to see how well your cat behaves. There are open breed classes for kittens but make sure your kitten is the right age for a given class on the day of the show. A kitten is considered to be an adult at nine months of age and can then compete in the open breed classes for adults. If you are a member of a club, you will find there are more classes to enter. And if you are a member of the club organising the show, you will get a reduction in fee for each class entered.

A week before the show, you should receive a numbered disc called a tally. The number on your tally will coincide with the number of the pen allocated to you. You will also receive passing-out and vetting cards for each of your entries.

Make sure you get your cat in 'show' condition well in advance. Take particular care of grooming. White cats usually need to be bathed several days before the show. Check for fleas. Long haired breeds need dusting with talcum powder. Liberally sprinkle into the coat and thoroughly brush out. This helps make the coat stand out. Ensure this is done several days before the show since residues of powder may get the cat disqualified. Thread your cat's tally on some white elastic and check that it fits comfortably round his neck.

When you take your cat to the show, he must be in an escape-proof container. You are not allowed to carry him in or have him on a collar or lead.

Vetting-in starts early in the morning. Your cat will be taken out of his basket and examined for fitness. He will be disqualified if he seems to be sickening for some diseases, has sore gums, dirty ears or fleas.

Once through the vetting you will have to put your cat in the pen bearing the same number as your tally. According to show rules, you must provide your own plain white sanitary tray and plain white basket. Litter is provided by the show organisers, but you must supply your own cat food. Before you put your cat in his pen, a final grooming is permitted but powdering is banned. I would advise you not to feed your cat before the judging.

A steward will take your cat out of the pen and place it on a table for the judge to examine. This continues until every class has been judged. As the show proceeds, award cards are put on the pens – red for first; blue for second; yellow for third. If there is to be a Best-in-Show, the judges will submit their nominations. In the afternoon, selected panels of judges will choose the best adult, kitten and neuter from each of the long haired, short haired, Siamese and Burmese classes.

Just think of the excitement if your cat happens to be one of the winners. But even if your cat never wins a prize, I am sure you will not be too disappointed. After all, he is still very special – your very own, much loved pet.

Useful Addresses

Health and Welfare

The Cats' Protection League
20 North Street, Horsham, West Sussex.

Feline Advisory Bureau
Honorary Secretary, 350 Upper
Richmond Road, Putney,
London, SW15.

Pet Health Council
4th Floor, Walter House, 418/422 Strand,
London, WC2R OPL.

RSPCA
The Causeway, Horsham, West Sussex.

PDSA
PDSA House, South Street, Dorking, Surrey.

Magazines

Cats
Watmoughs Ltd., Idle, Bradford,
West Yorkshire, BD10 8NL.

Cat World
Scan House, Southwick Street, Southwick,
Brighton, Sussex.